Holy *CRAP!* I'm Selling My Home. NOW WHAT?
The Home-Selling Guidebook

Rick Machle
Growing Ideas, LLC

Rick Machle

Holy CRAP! I'm Selling My Home. NOW WHAT? The Home-Selling Guidebook

Published by: Growing Ideas, LLC

Text design by: Rick Machle

Cover design by: Rick Machle

A CIP record for this book is available from the Library of Congress Cataloging-in-Publication Data

ISBN-13: 978-0-578-42776-8

Distributed by:

Growing Ideas, LLC

HomeSellingGuideBook.com

Dedicated to Sandy, Jazmine, Willa, Efis & Tosh who have made my house a home.

Table of Contents

Foreword

The phone rings. You answer. You are being transferred out of town. Or that amazing home that you've been watching just came on the market. Or you realize that your home is way too big, and it is time to downsize. You think, Holy Crap! I'm selling my home. Now what?

If you do not want to read or even buy this book, you simply need to hire a great real estate agent who will handle most of what is included in the following pages. However, you may still want to read this book because there is a chapter to help locate a good agent. You will also learn what to expect from that agent or the skills that you will need were you to sell your home on your own. While your cousin or that person you met in line at the grocery store may be a good agent, are you going to risk your most valuable asset on a hunch that he or she truly is? This book will give you some tips on determining the skills necessary to sell your home yourself, how reputable an agent is, how to price your home correctly, how to get your home ready for sale, and the different marketing tools that either you or your agent may utilize to let everyone know what makes your home special.

What is described in this book are the tasks that I have observed the best agents perform for their sellers. These help them sell their homes faster and for more money. Armed with this information, you will be able to guide your agent if he or she is less familiar with the tools and tips that it describes.

I am not a real estate agent but instead I have been a real estate photographer for over fifteen years. I have spoken to over one thousand agents. Over this time, certain themes and advice have consistently emerged. This book will let you know some of their guidance in a few hours instead of fifteen years.

Good. You are still here. You must be looking to avoid some of the errors I and others have made. The last time that my wife and I sold our home was before I was in the real estate industry. We wondered if we should sell it ourselves, and if not, who should we hire to help sell it? What should we do to get our home ready? What can we expect? What was the right price for our home? How long should it take? These are questions you may also have. Most people sell their homes about every 7 to 10 years. Like everything else in this world, this industry is constantly changing. Even if you sold your home a decade ago, much has changed.

When my wife and I were selling our home in a suburb of Denver, Colorado, the real estate market at the time was very hot. It should have sold in weeks—maybe a month or two. For twenty years prior to that time, I had experience in marketing businesses (both large and small), hotels, and some of the most prestigious resorts in the United States. I had been a successful business owner, professional photographer, video producer, and website developer. What I didn't know about was real estate. And of course, since I knew nothing about it, I made assumptions that turned out to be wrong.

When we were selling our home, I thought that every agent was the same as the next. I assumed that the agent would put my home in the multiple listing service or MLS. People see it. Someone buys it. Pretty simple right? Wrong. At the end of June that year, my wife and I went down to the small boutique real estate firm in the strip mall near our house, talked to an agent, and signed a listing agreement. I gave the agent the photographs. He did an open house, and that was it. It sat for months.

Did I mention it was a hot sellers' market where there were many more buyers than sellers? Back then, we didn't know much about pricing our home either. When it came to setting the price, we figured that since our neighbor had just sold, and because their house was smaller than ours, we should price ours higher than theirs—yet another mistake. While the market was hot, it was not quite as hot as when our neighbor sold their home. It turned out that we priced it too high.

After five months of little action and no offers, we decided to list with a different agent. Now it was late fall. Having not learned from our previous error, we didn't research the new agent any more than we had the first one. We thought perhaps this new agent would be more motivated or more effective. She might even have a secret buyer. She would do something miraculous that would sell our home. She didn't.

Before we listed our home in June, we had moved much of our furniture out of the home that we were selling into our new home. After going with the new agent, we thought that we'd take the remaining furniture out of our house. We thought that a buyer could see it as a blank slate, picturing their furniture in the home instead of ours. This was yet another mistake. I'm not sure why I thought that would be an effective strategy, as we had built our home after seeing a fully staged model. After eight months, we finally sold our house for about what our neighbors had sold theirs for. In hindsight, it appears that the only part of this process that we did correctly was to use the photographs that I had taken. The person who bought it, did so sight unseen, from the photos alone.

In summary, we chose the wrong agent twice, set the price incorrectly, took too long to reduce it, and removed all the furniture. Where was this book when we were selling our house? Well, now you can benefit from what I have learned.

Since that time, I have been creating websites, videos, 3-D tours, and photographing homes for real estate agents throughout Colorado. (RockinMedia.com) My company has taken photos of low-end "fixer uppers" all the way up to multimillion-dollar properties, including penthouse condos and some of the largest, most expensive estates. I've photographed homes and produced other media directly for homeowners, discount agents, and full-service agents. For a time, I was even a marketing director and part owner of a real estate firm.

I have had a front-row seat seeing what it takes to successfully sell a home for the most money. I have probably seen it all. I've also had the privilege of working with some of the best real estate agents in Colorado. I've talked to thousands of agents and listened to their stories and heard the mistakes that many homeowners have made. This book is designed to help you avoid the pitfalls by teaching you how to select the right real estate agent (if any) for you, price your home correctly, get it ready for sale, and market your home most effectively.

I'm not a real estate agent or mortgage broker. I'm not trying to sell you anything. No matter whether you decide to sell your home without an agent, use a discount agent or a full-service agent you will know what to expect. My goal is to share with you my insights. This book is designed to help you get more money from the sale of your home and to sell it faster. I do have one selfish goal. By following this guidebook, you might make my or another photographer's work easier. More importantly, by having your home ready to photograph when the photographer arrives, the better your home will look online, in print, and in person.

I've tried to keep this book short. After all, you have a home to sell. This book contains only the essentials as I see them for you to sell your home quickly.

I wish to thank all the agents who have shared their perspectives with me. I also want to thank my wife, Sandy, who has put up with this crazy industry and the amount of time it has taken away from us being together.

Throughout this book you'll find links that direct you to examples of the topic being discussed. I. If you're reading this as an e-book, you can click on the link itself, but photos on the web in a Kindle reader are not good quality, but it does work well in the Kindle app for tablet or phone. In the printed version of this book, type in the specific link or simply open any web browser, enter HCBookPics.com/examples, and go to each chapter.

Both the publisher and author have used their best efforts to prepare this information. No representations or warranties for its contents, either expressed or implied, are offered or allowed, and both parties disclaim any implied warranties of merchantability or fitness for your particular purpose. The advice and strategies presented herein may not be suitable for you or your situation. Consult with professional legal, accounting, and real estate advisors where and when appropriate. Neither the publisher nor author shall be liable for any loss of profit or any other damages, including but not limited to special, incidental, consequential, or punitive, arising from or relating to your reliance on this information.

Holy *CRAP!* I'm Selling My Home. NOW WHAT?

CHAPTER ONE

Overview

In order to sell your home, you need to market it. This means you need to take the appropriate steps to attract potential buyers. There's a separate sales process that includes finding buyers, negotiating a sales price, writing the contract, overcoming issues found during the inspections, resolving miscellaneous items, and closing the sale. While these tasks are essential, they are not covered in this book. This book aims at helping you to find the right agent to work with (if you don't want to sell it yourself), getting your home ready for sale, and marketing it so that the perfect buyer can find it. This is not a real estate sales-process book.

When it comes to marketing your home, the goal is to attract as many potential buyers as possible. This is done through high-quality photographs, a variety of real estate websites, videos, virtual tours, print materials, and purposeful use of social media platforms.

Selling your home begins with making it look its best. Some people believe that they can sell their home as is (especially in a strong sellers' market), while others have taken extraordinary measures to get their homes ready to sell.

Some agents and homeowners have done most everything

right, and more importantly for your sake, they have shared what they could have done better. You may live in a condo, townhouse, duplex, single-family home, row house, farm, cabin, estate, ranch, or any other type of residential property. To simplify the language in this book, the word "home" or "house" will be used when referring to any of these types of residential dwellings. Because each home and property is different, some of the recommendations will fit your situation; some may not. However, what is common to everyone is knowing the rules of the road.

CHAPTER TWO

Rick's Rules to Sell By

There are secrets to selling your home and still remaining sane. A great deal of this process has to do with your mind-set. Accept the following rules, and you will find the process much easier.

Rick's Rule 1: It's no longer your home. It's just a house.

As soon as you consider putting your home on the market, it's no longer your home. A home is a place that you live and make a life. A house is an asset that you sell for the most money. Think of your home as a large pile of cash. Whether you are asked to change the paint color or rearrange the furniture, you don't care. It's just four walls. Whatever makes it worth more.

In the industry the process of turning your home into a house is called "depersonalizing." You are trying to appeal to the broadest possible market. It goes beyond taking down everything that makes it "your home," like family photos, pet toys/beds/scratching posts, toiletries, and religious items. You want to make it a house that everyone wants to buy. Do not take the recommendations from an agent or stager personally. He or she is looking at your home from a buyer's perspective.

The sale of your house will be easier if you keep in mind

that people don't live in staged houses. You stage your house so that it will appeal to the buyer. Consider the word "staging." It implies that you are putting on a theatrical production. It's not the "real" world. Once you have done all the work that is described later in chapter 4, you may feel like there's no way you can live in this house. After all it doesn't even feel like your home anymore. Congratulations! You have achieved the goal.

It's no longer your home. It's just a house. In fact, from this point forward in this book we will not use the word "home" to refer to where you live. It's now simply a house. You want buyers to picture it as their home and not your house.

Rick's Rule 2: Nobody wants to buy a used house.

Of course, unless it's a newly built house, everyone knows that most houses have been previously lived in. Your job is to make your house to look as new as possible. Along with de-personalizing, you need to paint, dust, and clean. This rule also covers deodorizing your house so that it smells new. Make sure that pet hair and dreadful odors, such as that cat-box smell are also removed. It's important to keep in mind that some buyers or their children have pet allergies. If you have an opportunity, go to a builder's model home. You will never see dog hair or a dirty cat box. (hcbookpics.com/205).

Rick' Rule 3: The bigger it looks, the more it's worth.

Since most people don't live in a staged house, what's the secret to making yours look like one? The more stuff in your house, the smaller it will look. Alternatively, the less cluttered it is, the bigger it will look. This rule could also be called "Half and Half." If you are like most people, you will want to go into a specific room and remove half of the items, and then go back and remove half of the remaining items that are still there. You may want to remove less than half of the larger pieces of furniture in a room, but for most people, the rule for everything else remains. For example, in the kitchen, remove half of the items that are on your counters. Then remove half of those items that still remain. (hcbookpics.com/210).

Rick's Rule 4: A vacant house is a sad and lonely house.

This is the mirror image of Rick's Rule 3. While you don't want too many items in your house, and you don't want too few either. You want to make your house look as big as possible by not having too much stuff, but you also want it to seem warm, friendly, and welcoming by not having too few things. There needs to be a balance. Most people have a hard time sizing a room. Will their couch fit along your living room wall? Can their king-sized bed fit in your master bedroom? Will their table work in the dining room? Is their pool table too big for your rec room? If you remove all the furniture, your buyer will not be able to gauge these concerns. (hcbookpics.com/215).

Secondly, a vacant house does not feel like a place your buyer can call home. There is a reason that most builders will stage their new houses: to make them feel more welcoming for potential buyers.

Rick's Rule 5: It doesn't matter what you paid.

When it comes to selling your house the amount of money you invested to improve your house is not important in this process. What matters is how much someone else will pay you for those upgrades. This is really the market's rule because the market rules. For example, the kitchen that you renovated a couple years ago that cost you $35,000 may only return $10,000. Another example could be that you paid $250,000 for your house ten years ago and put in $50,000 for a new basement and back deck. Your house should be worth at least $300,000, right? The short answer is yes— but only if you can find a buyer willing to pay that amount.

Keep in mind that your buyer may be willing to pay the $300,000, but the appraisal may come in at $270,000. The bank will only loan $270,000, so the buyer will need to come up with an additional $30,000 in cash for the sale to close.

In addition, it also does not matter what you owe, want or need to gain from the proceeds of the sale of your house. You may have an eye on that great house where you need $40,000 for the down payment. After paying off the loan on your current house you will need to sell for $280,000 to net $40,000. After your house goes on the market, you find that the highest offer is $265,000. Unless you are in a booming real estate market, holding out for that additional $15,000, may require you to wait much longer than you originally anticipated, and now that dream home you have been watching is under contract. During the downturn of 2008, many people owed more on their houses than they were worth, or they were "upside down" on their mortgages. In parts of the US home values dropped to less than half what they owed on their mortgages. Over ten years later, some people still owe more on their houses than they could sell them for.

There is a flip side to this rule. It is one that sellers typically do not mind. In a strong seller's market, your house may be appreciating so quickly that you could see the cost of improvements being recouped in a few years or sometimes months. For a period of time in Denver, prices were appreciating about 10 percent a year, so a home worth $350,000 in one year would be worth $385,000 the next and over $423,000 the year after that.

CHAPTER THREE

For Sale by Owner? Or Hire an Agent?

Now that you are ready to get started, you need to determine whether you are going to sell your house yourself or you plan to hire an agent. If you decide to hire an agent, will you use a full-service agent or a discount agent? These questions can affect the entire process, including how much work you will have to do yourself to get your house sold.

Selling It Yourself

You may be considering selling the house without an agent. You may have heard this called FSBO (pronounced "fizzbo") or For Sale by Owner. A recent National Association of Realtors survey found that less than 10 percent of sellers elected to sell their houses without agents.

Selling it yourself can save you the cost of commission. Perhaps you are in a sellers' market where there are multiple buyers for every seller. Many houses have multiple offers and go under contract within a few days or a week. Your house could go under contract in a matter of days without an agent. This can be done by selling it yourself with limited or no marketing. Just remember that putting it under contract is far from getting it closed. Once your house is under contract there is still a ton of work yet to be done.

Have you heard the saying "A person who represents him- or herself has a fool for a client?" While this is usually applied to a court defendant who acts as his or her own attorney, it can also be applied to real estate. There are too many potential unknowns that could arise during your sales process (or lost sale). When you combine the unpredictably of circumstances with the possibility of under or over pricing your house, it may not be worth the amount you save in commission when selling without an agent.

Selling your house by yourself requires you to do an honest evaluation of the skills that you possess. The following is a partial list of tasks you will need to be prepared to do. Because you are doing it yourself, you will be responsible for all the labor usually done by an agent.

1. What are you going to set the price at? Are you pricing it correctly for the market? How do you know? If it sells faster than you expected, did you price it too low, leaving money on the table? If you are too high, how will you know that? How long will you stay at the current price if you are not seeing action?

2. Are you going to stage it yourself? If not, whom will you hire? How much does that cost? If you do it yourself, is there someone to give you a second opinion as to what changes you should make to your house?

3. Who will photograph your house? How will you locate a high-quality real estate photographer? How much will it

cost? Do you want aerial photos? Do you want twilight photos? Will your photographer shoot single exposure or HDR?

4. How will buyers get into your house for showings? Will you be there for showings? Will you have a lockbox? What are the showing instructions? How will you communicate those instructions to buyers or their agents?

5. Are you the best person to negotiate the price or other issues when the buyer may have an experienced negotiator working on his or her behalf?

6. During the inspection process items are found that need to be negotiated. Can you handle the negotiation?

7. Now that inspection issues have been negotiated, do you have a list of contractors who can quickly fix issues that were found, so that they do not delay the sale?

8. Who is going to meet with the appraiser? What if the appraisal comes in lower than expected? How will you negotiate with the buyer?

9. Often a buyer hits a snag in financing a week before you are due to close. Are you going to have a solution so that it will still close, or will you have to start the process over again with a different buyer?

10. What if you miss something, either during contract negotiations or on the back end, that you don't even foresee as an issue? What you don't know can hurt you or postpone your closing. Here is an example. The buyers thought that your washer and dryer and refrigerator were included because you didn't specifically

exclude them. You get to the closing table, and the buyers mention that they are so excited about having that high-end, French-door refrigerator. You tell them that it wasn't included. Their agent asks you where it specifically stated that. That omission just cost you $4,000. This is only one small example.

11. Who will write the contracts and deal with contingencies? If you decide to sell your house yourself, you will need to hire an attorney. Who will you hire? How much will that cost?

Of course, there are some exceptions to when it could make sense for you to sell your house without an agent. Perhaps you have a friend who wants to buy your two-year-old house, and it's a cash transaction without inspections. Or perhaps you are selling the house to your child or children. Because price is less critical, you are not necessarily looking to make the most money from the house. They will already know the condition of the house, and may want to buy as-is. In these types of situations, you are not necessarily looking to make the most money from the house, so the price is less critical. You may however want to hire a real estate attorney to handle all the contracts.

Discount Agent or Full-Service Agent

In many markets today, you can find an agent willing to sell your house for a discount. There are two different types within this category. The first is an agent or company willing to work for a fixed fee. The second type will charge a percentage of the sale price, but it's discounted from the standard, full-service agent's fee. The full-service agent will often charge more than the other two, but how much he or she charges you can be negotiated.

Flat-Fee Discount Companies/Agents

In most cases the agent or company that will list your house for a flat-fee will reduce your commission cost. If you decide to select a flat-fee company, you will want to know what is and is not included in their fee. You may still have to handle some of the items in the "selling it yourself" section of this chapter. Many of the services that other agents provide may cost additional fees. Ask whether they will handle issues that may come up along the way. I've heard of a seller showing up to the closing table looking for his agent. He asks the buyer's agent where his representative is. The answer was "nowhere"—they didn't have one. They were on their own.

Something to keep in mind with a company that lists your house for a flat fee is that many of them will also pay a flat fee to the buyer's agent. This fee is substantially below what the buyer's agent would be paid through a standard commission structure. Be sure you clarify this. A buyer's agent will know what he or she will be paid for selling your house because it's in the notes on your house. All things being equal between your house and another house for sale, the agent may direct the buyer to the other house, where a standard commission is being paid. Many buyers' agents will negotiate with their buyers that anything less than their standard commission will be paid by the buyer. This becomes a disincentive for the buyer to purchase your house. If you know this up front, you could also agree to pay the standard buyer's agent commission.

A house that I recently photographed had been listed by a discount broker who took his own photos and put the listing in the MLS. That was in the early part of the summer. By the time the seller changed to a full-service agent, it was late August. In most US markets, the buyer pool is much smaller at the end of the summer than at the beginning. The loss of those months makes the hypothetical $6,600 difference in commission look small in comparison to still owning a property worth over $300,000. The delay forced the seller to lower the listing price by $10,000.

Discount or Full-Service Agent

It is important to understand that the company for which an agent works does not determine whether he or she is a discount or full-service agent. It is essential to research the services provided by each individual agent. There are agents who give a full-service, high-end experience who work for a firm that is typically known as a discount company. Alternatively, there are agents who do the bare minimum who work for companies known for providing a full-service experience. Agents are typically independent contractors and can make their own decisions about how much or little work they put into selling your house. Therefore, it is crucial to research the specific agent you are hiring, and not just the company they are working for.

You may be asking why you would pay a full 6 percent (or

more) commission. Let's discuss a little bit about commissions. You may have heard that most agents charge a 4, 5, or 6 percent commission. About half that percentage goes to the buyer's agent. Your agent would only get the full 6 percent if he or she brings the buyer to your house as well. Normally, agents will earn about half of the total commission for listing your house. As the seller, you will be paying both the listing and buyer's agent commission.

The commission that's discussed here refers to the listing agent's commission. When you look at the amount of the listing commission, it can still give you sticker shock. It can seem like quite a bit of money. Remember all those tasks that you would have to do if you sold your house alone? Since a quality agent will take on most, if not all, of those tasks, the commission begins to look fair and reasonable. Part of that commission goes to the company the agent works for to cover its general operating costs. And much of the agent's income goes toward running his or her own small business. Agents need to cover all the associated costs that come with running a business, including insurance, continuing education, and licensing fees. The agent also has direct costs related to marketing your property. And of course, the agent also has the time he/she spends selling your house.

In addition, unless they negotiate something different with you, agents are on a 100 percent commission structure. The agent does not get paid until you sell—even if you elect to take your house off the market. In fact, in this case an agent will have invested a lot of time and money to market your house that he/she will not recoup.

The commission for the listing side of the transaction usually correlates to the amount of work that the listing agent does or doesn't do on your behalf. A discounted commission usually means decreased service (or you are a good friend or family member). Better marketing and network connections can lead to your house being seen by more agents and buyers which can lead to a higher selling price. In the marketing chapter of this book, you'll learn some of the tools that an agent can use or can elect not use to sell your house. However, why would you expect him or her to do expend all their means to sell your house when you are looking to pay them less than they are worth? Don't be surprised when the agent says to you, "I can cut my commission, but what part of my marketing program do you not want me to implement?" You should not expect to get everything for less.

It's true that you could possibly save money on the commission by working with a discount agent. It's like selling your house on your own. What you may end up discovering is that the net amount in your pocket at the end of the sale may be less with a discount agent versus a full-service agent. On the flip side, by marketing your house more thoroughly, the full-service agent could get you a higher sales price for your house versus the discount agent. Here's an example: you put your house on the market for $300,000. The discount agent at 1 percent would cost you $3,000 in listing commission. A full-service agent may cost you $9,600 in commission. That's a difference of $6,600. However, through networking and other marketing programs by the full-service agent he/she is able to bring you more buyers and multiple offers. This ups the bidding the price, resulting in a final sale price of $320,000. In the end, you are walking away with a net gain of over $10,000 more with the full-service broker, even after the higher commission cost. And remember that the commission is only paid at closing. Always consider the net amount that you take away from the sale verses the cost of commission.

All agents will put your house in the MLS. If the brokerage firm or MLS has a distribution agreement with other sites, your house will then be syndicated to other major real estate websites like Zillow®, Trulia®, and realtor.com®. Getting your house on the web is a good start, but the full-service agents with whom I work do much more for their sellers. As previously mentioned, how much service you get is not dependent on which company holds the agent's license. Additional marketing implemented by your agent can lead to more buyers and a higher selling price.

The size of the firm the agent works for can also be important. Smaller firms have smaller networks of agents to spread the word about your house. There are some firms where individual offices can have over one hundred agents. When your house is discussed in a sales meeting, you now have many more agents who can bring in potential buyers. Some offices even have office tours of all the homes they are listing. The more agents in the know, the more exposure your house has.

Rick Machle

Finding the Right Agent—Not All Agents Are the Same

Now that you know the different types of agents, how do you find the right agent for you? Some agents will recommend minor changes to your house, while others will completely stage your house by bringing in their own furniture and other items to augment what is in your house. Some other agents have put on garage sales for sellers who are out of town. Many agents will showcase your house in real estate magazines, on the best websites, and even on TV. Some agents have people to handle all the paperwork, so that they can concentrate on finding the perfect buyer for your house. Some work in boutique real estate firms, while others are in large companies with vast national and international marketing. If you are selling a luxury house, this could be critical to finding the right buyer.

As mentioned earlier, agents are affiliated with companies but are independent contractors. Each has his or her own independent business. Some are individual agents, others are partnerships, and still others are in groups both small and large. Some agents only work in the industry part- time. They are content with selling one or two houses a year. Others are only happy when spending 100 hours a week. They like working with both sellers and buyers and sell tens of millions of dollars of real estate a year. Some are new to the industry (especially in a hot market), while others have been selling real estate for decades. Some prefer to work with buyers, others with sellers. It's important for you to know the type of agent and qualifications of the person you are hiring.

Treat the hiring of your agent like you are an employer conducting an interview. You should ask for references and talk to people within your neighborhood or community. Many agents sell in specific neighborhoods, so you can ask other neighbors for their impressions. Fortunately, agents have their signs in front of the houses they are listing making them easy to find. The website for the company the agent works for often has an agent page or section for each agent. On that page you can find other houses the agent is currently listing. Try contacting those homeowners to learn more about their experience with this particular agent.

Interview Questions

You have decided to hire an agent. Selecting the right person could make or cost you thousands of additional dollars and save or cost you lots of time. The first step you should take is to interview multiple agents—even if one of them is a relative of yours. After all, who doesn't have one in their family? You may want to talk to him or her last. Then you will have a better idea of what other information you need to know.

Start the interview process by walking the agent around the property. Tell the agent special features of your house— what you like most.

1) What changes should I make before I putting my house on the market?

Of the thousands of houses that I have photographed, I can count on two hands the number of houses that didn't need something improved before going on the market. Most could still use even more work by the time I show up to take photos. Regardless of whether you intend to implement any of the recommendations, an agent should have some—even if it's to put away the toothpaste and other toiletries.

It's a red flag when an agent tells you to put it on the market immediately and that he or she wouldn't change a thing. There are two reasons an agent might say this. First, they perceive the market is changing in a downward direction, and if you take time to do minor changes, it could cost you time and perhaps money that you don't have. Even so, the agent should explain this and give you a list of small items that should be taken care of or put away to make the spaces look bigger and better.

The second reason that a less-than-scrupulous agent might not recommend changes is that he or she is anxious to get you to sign the listing agreement. Even if your house's current condition is less than optimal, it could sell quickly enough, especially if the agent were to price it to sell fast. With a little effort, it could sell for more. For instance, you're working with a discount agent who is only charging you a 1 percent commission. You may need to spend a couple of weeks and $1,000 to get the house ready to sell by fixing the gate, painting, and replacing the front door hardware. By making these changes, you're able to get $5,000 more for you house. A 1 percent commission will only result in a $50 increase in the agent's commission. Your net loss would be $3,950—even including the commission.

Higher Sale Price	$5,000.00
Cost of Repairs	$1,000.00
Additional Commission	<u>$50.00</u>
Additional Income from Sale	$3,950.00

2) How much experience do you have?

Agents are required to learn information to get licensed. This gives agents the core knowledge they need to minimize potential issues that come along in what can often be a complex selling process. However, like most other professions, there's no substitute for experience. If your agent has seen it before, he or she is much more likely to be able to solve it or head it off even before it becomes an issue.

3) What price should I list my house for?

If an agent tells you a price right then and there, ask how he or she came up with that price. The agent might say that he or she has sold lots of houses around you. This could be a warning sign that the agent is pulling the price from... you-know-where. Ask if the agent can show you the comps (comparable listings).

Professional agents should give you a CMA or Competitive Market Analysis. This will show you in detail what comparable houses have sold for, where they are located, how they differ from your house, and how many have sold in each period of time, as well as other market conditions, including average sale price and days on market. When it comes to price, it not only matters what city you are in, but also the neighborhood or even which street on which you live. It may be a good sign if the agent indicates that he or she needs to get back with you with a price; the agent needs to do some homework.

Beware of the agent who appeals to your sense of greed. "Wow, the last agent told me my house was worth $20,000 less than you say I should list it for!" The price stated may be higher than other the agents, but the first amount may be a more realistic market price. If you list too high, you could waste valuable selling time.

4) Who will photograph my house?

This is a good indicator of the agent's overall profession-alism and how much he or she plans to spend for market-ing. If the agent says something like, "This market is so hot that I will just take them with my phone," then this person is not a real estate professional who is willing to do the minimum, let alone the maximum to market your house.

Understand that well over 95 percent of buyers start their searches online, so quality photos are essential to showing your house in its best light. You don't think it's that impor-tant? Start searching for houses online. You'll instantly be able to tell professional photographs from ones taken on the homeowner's or agent's phones. In the past, the cost of photography was very high, but today an agent should be able to get professional, high-quality HDR photographs for around $300.

5) What will you do to sell my house?

The agent should have a specific process that he or she can clearly state as to what steps will be taken to get your house ready, market it, and handle offers. The more services the agent provides, the less you will need to do yourself.

6) Have you sold other houses in this neighborhood?

Selling a house also involves selling the community as well. The more familiar the agent is with your area, the better he or she can market your house. The agent can describe the great features of local parks, shopping, and school districts.

7) Have you had an issue come up in a recent house that you've listed? If so, how did you deal with it?

Agents should have a story or two to tell you. Not all deals go smoothly. Some may, but there are often issues with a buyer, inspections, the appraisal, or the loan closing on time. How he or she handled these issues will indicate the level of expertise and connections the agent has in regards to selling your home.

8) How much of this process will you personally be handling?

Some agents have a person who handles the marketing, and a different person to shepherd the transaction. Some agents handle all or most of the transactions themselves. Neither is better than the other, provided they are reliable. You may personally prefer one over the other. You will know that to expect. You won't be surprised if you are working primarily with the other team members instead of the agent. The agent may instead be spending his or her time looking for qualified buyers. Other agents may prefer to control the entire process. You may be the only client the agent is working for so that he or she can devote all their time and effort to you.

9) If you are unavailable, who will be handling the sale of my house?

The answer is somewhat obvious for teams or partnerships. Other individual agents have informal relationships with another agent or agents to cover for them when they are unavailable. You need to know this so that you are not surprised later in the process.

Sorting Out Competing Offers

In the welcome event that you receive multiple offers, you will want an agent who has the experience to review the offers and point out the pros and cons of each. Not all offers are created equal. Some buyers come with low-offer prices but are cash buyers. Others may have higher-price offers but include special considerations or contingencies, such as their house needs to sell first before they can buy yours. Still others may offer you the price that you are looking for but have yet to be approved by their lenders. A good real estate agent will walk you through each offer to give you the best outcome.

Closing the Sale

A successful closing begins as soon as you are under contract. After you are under contract, your agent will start dealing with the many issues that can derail the sale. Not every issue that comes up (like getting final loan approval) can be managed by the agent. With luck you will have a backup offer, were that to occur. There are other hurdles that a quality real estate agent can help you overcome. These usually have to do with items found during the inspection or appraisal.

Something that you should consider when selecting an agent may seem obvious yet is often overlooked. Do you like the person who will be selling your house? You may buy furniture or even a car or many other products or services from someone that you don't like. In this case you should like and trust the person who is selling your house. Why is this? To begin with, this person will be going through every nook and cranny of your house. If the agent has the "ick" factor, you're probably not going to want him or her doing that. The agent will also need to know some of your personal financial information. One of the most important reasons for liking your agent is that you could be working with this person for months, and with more expensive houses and certain market conditions, even years.

In addition, does this person present himself or herself professionally? This is someone who will be negotiating one of the most—if not the most—expensive assets that you own. Do you really want someone representing you who does not have a professional appearance? This is everything from how the agent dresses, how he or she speaks, and even whether the agent respects your house enough to remove shoes when entering. Is this the best person to take your house to the next stage?

Holy *CRAP!* I'm Selling My Home. NOW WHAT?

CHAPTER FOUR

Taking Your House to the Next Stage

Think back to a first romantic date that you had in the past. I'm sure at the time, you combed your hair, took a shower, shaved, put on nice clothes and clean underwear, and perhaps even trimmed or pluck your eyebrows. You may have even purchased a new outfit or pair of shoes to impress your date.

Now, perhaps you have been in a long-term relationship. You probably shave less frequently, walk around the house in your sweatpants and holey T-shirt, and forget about the underwear.

If you're like me, the current condition of your house is more similar to that person in a long-term relationship than someone going on a first date. It's time to get your house in first-date condition. It's time to make your house look its best. As you go through each space, you will want to review what should be replaced, removed, or repaired.

One way to save time reading this chapter is to hire a real estate agent who will either hire a stager or who can make suggestions of changes that you can make—or even stage your house him/herself. Even if the agent is planning on staging, you will probably need to do some of these tasks yourself. Another shortcut to understanding the look you will want to achieve is to visit high-end builders' model homes in your area. As an alternative, you can visit different builders' websites to see how they stage their houses. These builders spend thousands, and sometimes hundreds of thousands, of dollars researching what will help sell their houses. This is because they must sell ten or more of the same house in the same neighborhood, so their models have to be perfect. Here's the shortcut. If you don't see it in the model, you probably want to remove it from your house as well. When you go to one of these model houses, you never see shampoo in the showers, medicine on the counter tops in the powder room, or dog bowls in the kitchen. And of course, you never see dirty laundry in the closets or the laundry room. You can see where all the rooms were professionally staged at hcbookpics.com/400.

On many occasions I have photographed the same house at various stages of staging. In this example the various stages being; vacant, basic staging, complete staging during the holidays, and complete staging without holiday decorations (hcbookpics.com/401). After the last staging was initiated, the house sold very quickly.

You may need to stage your home with new furniture. While your furniture may have been contemporary when you first purchased it out of college, now, thirty years later it might not have the same appeal. The cat's used the easy chair for a scratching post, and your seventy-five-pound dog has left a permanent imprint in the couch. The area rug in the living room looks like it has been on a shop floor. This is when it is worth changing out your furniture with staging furniture. See the difference.(hcbookpics.com/405)

Instead of changing out your furniture, you may simply need to rearrange it to make the room appear more spacious. Your living room layout works well for you now when you want to play video games, but you may find there's a more effective orientation the way the agent or stager wants to move furniture around.

The goal of staging is to make a buyer say "Wow!" when he or she first enters your house and subsequently when the buyer steps into each room.

You will also want to reset your rooms to their original purposes. Change what is intended to be the formal dining room that you have been utilizing as a playroom back into a dining room. It's usually quite clear from the layout that it should have been a dining room. Remember, people have difficulty imagining what the room should be if it currently being used for a different purpose.

Staging your house will make it look its best so that it sells faster. What follows is a check list for various rooms like bathrooms, living room, kitchen, and bedrooms. You may not have all these rooms in your house. Congratulations! Less work to be done!

A professional stager may look at the different staging lists in this chapter and say, "it doesn't include this or it doesn't include that". The stager would be right, but unless you hire a professional stager, this list will be a great start and put you ahead of almost everyone else on the market.

CAUTION: Know your limitations, and take care not to injure yourself. Hire the appropriate professional to complete tasks that you are unable to handle safely.

While lit candles and fireplaces can give spaces in your house a warm feeling, never leave them unattended.

Staging can be a matter of triage. If you must get your house on the market in a week, the tasks you can get accomplished by yourself will be far fewer than if you have months. Too often people take on more than can be accomplished in the time they have available. If you have a week, don't take on a bathroom renovation; simply tidy it up and replace the shower curtain. What's worse than a dated bathroom? An unfinished bathroom. Also, anticipate that contractors may not to finish on time. It is common for flooring contractors to promise to come tomorrow and then call that morning and indicate that they will not be able to make it for ten days. Depending on the time of year, those ten days of lost marketing can be costly.

At the macro level, here are staging priorities based on the time and money available:

1. Declutter.
2. Clean.
3. Purchase new bedding, towels, rugs, pillows, etc.
4. Minor repairs like caulking, changing outdated faucets, or replacing door/drawer handles.
5. Major repairs like a kitchen renovation, new flooring, finishing the basement, or a new roof.

Remember that if you plan on taking on major repairs, complete those first before cleaning. In other words, do the priorities listed above in the reverse order.

The following basic tasks should be done, no matter the type or size of your house. When appropriate, tasks like vacuuming and washing windows are duplicated in each room. Keeping in mind the law of gravity, the tasks are generally ordered from the highest point in each room to the lowest. Save yourself from sweeping the floors twice - once before and one after cleaning the counters.

You can also download and print a PDF version of this checklist at hcbookpics.com/checklist.

- ☐ Dust lights and ceiling fans.
- ☐ Make sure all light bulbs match and are working.
- ☐ Wash windows.
- ☐ Dust window blinds.
- ☐ Confirm that all window blinds and curtains function properly.
- ☐ Vacuum curtains and window blinds.
- ☐ Remove personal photographs.
- ☐ Remove valuable artwork, jewelry, and other items that you may not want people to see online or steal during an open house.
- ☐ Replace personal photos with "neutral" artwork.
- ☐ Paint rooms in neutral colors.
- ☐ Remove religious symbols.
- ☐ Remove all signs of pets, including scratching posts, and hair balls (vacuum well).

☐ Dust and clean all television sets.
☐ Vacuum.
☐ Mop the floors.
☐ Stretch carpet.

Exterior—Front

Whether it's your buyer's first impression or what's called "curb appeal," the front of your house is critical to getting them to come in. People's initial reactions to your house will go a long way to whether they even step through the front door or move on. (hcbookpics.com/420) Rick's Rule 1 applies here as well. You may like all the bushes and trees being overgrown. After all, that's what gives you privacy from the street or your neighbors. While this may be true, it may also make the yard look unattended. It can also make it difficult to see your house. Being able to see your house is important, both in person and in photos online. If buyers can't see the house through the trees and shrubs, how can they judge whether your house should be their home?

- ☐ Clean gutters.
- ☐ Trim trees to make house more visible.
- ☐ Trim bushes to make house more visible.
- ☐ Rake leaves.
- ☐ Mow lawn.
- ☐ Edge lawn.
- ☐ Wash siding to remove dirt (be careful of older paint).
- ☐ Wash garage door.
- ☐ Paint as needed.
- ☐ Seal (or grade if unpaved) driveway.
- ☐ Fix concrete that may have settled.
- ☐ Shovel snow from walkways, steps, and driveway.
- ☐ During spring/summer, add flowering plants.
- ☐ Make sure any water features are functioning and clean (if in season).
- ☐ Remove storage pod(s) before photography and showings.
- ☐ Remove disabled vehicles from in front of your house or in the driveway.

Front Door/Porch/Patio

Even if you live in a condo or townhouse, you need to pay attention to how people feel as they come up to the front door. Your homeowners' association or complex may limit what you can do to your foyer, but even with these limits, there are many touches you can make. This is where your buyer will get the initial impression of how you've maintained the house. These can include little things like cobwebs or dirt or bigger issues like chipped paint. (hcbookpics.com/425)

One item that is often overlooked is the hardware on the front door. That twenty-year-old doorknob is now peeling, and the dead bolt and lock are sticky. Image walking up to your house as a new buyer. It's hot, and the kids are antsy because yours is the fifth house they have toured. The real estate agent tries to turn the key but can't get the door open. The agent turns it one direction and then the other. It turns, but he or she still can't open the door. Finally, the agent pulls on the door while turning the key, and it opens. What does this do to your first impression? When we photograph houses, we find this is too often the case. It especially happens in suburban houses. These homeowners usually enter the house through the garage and almost never use the front door. While this is understandable, you need to remember that unless you're going to have new buyers enter through the garage, you need to have the front door working properly.

☐ Remove cobwebs.

☐ Paint as needed.

☐ Wash to remove dirt.

☐ Stain or seal the wood or concrete.

☐ Add a place to sit.

☐ Add colorful outdoor pillows to sitting area.

☐ Place appropriately sized plants around porch or exterior entryway.

☐ During spring/summer, add a flowering plant.

☐ Shovel snow/ice from walkway.

☐ Be sure that cracks and settled steps are corrected.

Closets, Pantry, Storage Rooms, Garage & Sheds

Before you go inside and start looking at specific rooms, let's remember a nearly universal need. Nearly everyone wants to have places to store stuff. You want your house to appear like there is plenty of storage. This is done by minimizing items in your closets and other areas where you store your stuff. You don't want closets and the pantry to be totally empty but instead look like there is still plenty of room for more items. (hcbookpics.com/430)

This is an opportunity to start your move even before you are under contract. Rent a storage container or space and depending on the number of items that you will throw away, Bagster™ or roll-off dumpster. This is also an opportunity to assist those less fortunate by donating clothes and other items. If your budget is tight, you may want to dedicate one space to move all of your "Half and Half" items. This could be a storage room or the garage. You may not have either. In this case, purchase same-size boxes and neatly stack them in a spare room like a bedroom or loft.

Much of this chapter is dedicated to implementing Rick' Rule 3: Bigger is Worth More. As with the rooms and spaces in your home, you will want to remove half of the items in your closets, storage rooms, garage & pantry, and then remove another half of the remaining stuff.

For storage rooms and the garage, you should simply empty them out and clean them. These are two spaces where an empty space is NOT a lonely space. Empty storage and a clean garage makes buyers happy!

Entryway or Foyer

When you walk through your front door, what do you see? Often there are shoes and coats strewn everywhere. Sometimes there's a dog leash hanging up, and the light looks dated. That's fine if it's a 1920's Tudor. It's not so good if it's a 1990's builder-grade brass-and-glass light. (hcbookpics.com/435)

- ☐ Oil the door hinges to remove squeaks.
- ☐ Dust entry light (replace as needed).
- ☐ Remove coats from coat racks.
- ☐ Clear out the coat closet, leaving hangers for buyers' coats (you want them to stay).
- ☐ Remove fingerprints from door and frame.
- ☐ Clean light switches.
- ☐ Make sure all light bulbs match and are working
- ☐ Vacuum the floor.

Living Room—Family Room

Whether you have a living room, family room, or great room (or all of the above), these spaces are used for gathering. They need to reflect that purpose. When you enter this space, you'll want to look for a focal point. This could be a fireplace, bay window, standard window, or flat-screen TV. Perhaps you don't have any of these. Create your own focal point. That could be a nice coffee table or an interesting piece of wall art or a sculpture. You might set a flowing plant or bouquet of flowers on a coffee table. It's that focal point that photographers tend to look for when shooting your living space. (hcbookpics.com/440)

Arrange your furniture around that focal point. Keep in mind that part of that space should be seen as a place for people to sit and talk. It's not necessary to have all your furniture at right angles to the walls. Sometimes you can make a room look larger by angling the furniture.

- [ ] Arrange furniture around the focal point.
- [ ] Angle furniture relative to the walls.
- [ ] Minimize furniture.
- [ ] Remove half of half of items.
- [ ] Dust tables, other flat surfaces, lamps, bookshelves, and other items.
- [ ] Remove religious or political books.
- [ ] Place real estate magazines on the tables.
- [ ] Place small plants on one or two tables.
- [ ] Add flowers.
- [ ] Place a small plant on the coffee table.
- [ ] Add pillows (preferably new or newer).
- [ ] Add a throw over the couch.
- [ ] Cover the couch or chairs if they are very worn.
- [ ] Make sure that the pilot light in the gas-fireplace is lit and fireplace functions.
- [ ] Make sure all light bulbs match and are working.
- [ ] Clean light switches.
- [ ] Vacuum the floor.

Dining Room

Many houses have separate dining rooms. Others simply have dining spaces. Still others have an eat-in area in the kitchens that is used for dining. The purpose of staging a dining room is to make it appear as large as possible. Sometimes that means putting a leaf in the table to make it appear as though you can seat eight to ten guests, and sometimes it means removing a leaf to make the table look smaller and the room larger. (hcbookpics.com/445)

What you really want is for the dining area to be a place where people can imagine family and friends gathering during the holidays, or at parties or special events. People also want to visualize their families or friends sitting around the table and talking about the day's events.

To accomplish this goal, you need to make sure the chairs are in good working condition, so that when someone sits down to get a feel for what it's like to sit in this space, he or she won't feel like chair will collapse.

- ☐ Clean off the table.
- ☐ Make sure that chairs are dusted and clean.
- ☐ Use new place mats.
- ☐ Set the table with your best dinnerware and flatware.
- ☐ Add plant or flowers to the center of the table.
- ☐ Add candles (not lit) to your table.
- ☐ Set a tasteful and modest centerpiece in the center of the table; a small plant may be appropriate.
- ☐ Clean light switches.
- ☐ For photographs, remove high chair(s)
- ☐ Make sure all light bulbs match and are working.
- ☐ Vacuum the floor.

Kitchen

When it comes to selling your house, your kitchen is going to be one of the most important spaces. You want to make sure that it looks as new, fresh, and as clean as possible (Rick's Rule 2: Nobody wants to buy a used house). Your kitchen is a location where stuff tends to collect. No matter how much counter top space you have, you are going to want to make it appear larger. This is accomplished by Rick's Rule 3 or the half-half rule, where you take half of the appliances and other items from your counter tops, and then you remove another half. Some agents will recommend removing everything. I believe that this makes it look more like a vacant house instead of a house that's lived in but has plenty of storage. (hcbookpics.com/450)

Speaking of storage, you'll want to also use the half-half Rule 3 here too. Remove half of the items in your cabinets and pantry, and then remove half of the remaining items. When it's time for showings or photographs to be taken, you will also want to remove pet dishes. Many people have pet allergies, and some are cat people, while others are dog people. You don't want to drive away a potential buyer because of your pets.

- ☐ Clean light switches.
- ☐ Be sure appliances are in good working order and clean.
- ☐ Clean outside of appliances.
- ☐ Empty or remove trash can.
- ☐ Clean inside of refrigerator.
- ☐ Clean oven.
- ☐ Replace stove drip pans.
- ☐ Clean inside of microwave.
- ☐ Clean the sink.
- ☐ Wipe down counters.
- ☐ Clean disposal switch.
- ☐ Half-and-half the counter tops and island.
- ☐ Remove photos and other items from front and sides of refrigerator.
- ☐ Remove items stored on top of refrigerator.
- ☐ Half-and-half the cabinets.
- ☐ Half-and-half the pantry (if you have one).
- ☐ Clean the fronts of the cabinets.
- ☐ Clean the wall behind the stove.
- ☐ Clean the backsplash.
- ☐ Clean hood front and underneath.
- ☐ Make sure hood light works.

Holy *CRAP!* I'm Selling My Home. NOW WHAT?

- ☐ Replace dated or worn counter tops.
- ☐ Place a bowl with green apples or other <u>fresh </u>fruit on the counter or island.
- ☐ Make sure under-cabinet lights are working.
- ☐ Remove small appliances except for a coffee maker.
- ☐ Update door and drawer hardware with current style.
- ☐ Replace dated faucets.
- ☐ If needed, replace the bulb in the under-cabinet lighting and the microwave night-light.
- ☐ If you have a screen door out to a patio or deck, be sure that it's in good working order and screen is in good condition.
- ☐ Make sure all light bulbs match and are working.
- ☐ Remove rugs.
- ☐ Vacuum the floor.
- ☐ Mop the floor.

Bedrooms

Most of us spend about a one-third of a twenty-four-hour period in our bedrooms, and many of us spend more than half of our time at home in our bedrooms. Buyers will spend a great deal of time scrutinizing your bedrooms. You will not be able to do anything about many of the features they will be looking at. These include ceiling height and overall size, but there are other features you can modify to make the rooms look more spacious and inviting.

Master Bedroom

The master bedroom is usually the largest bedroom. Sometimes it has an en-suite bathroom, but not always. Many master bedrooms have sitting areas, while others have gas fireplaces. Some even have a private deck. The master bedroom needs to be warm, cozy, and free of clutter. Imagine you've been out on a long day of house shopping, and your house is the last one your buyers walk into. Wouldn't it be wonderful if they walk into your master bedroom and feel like if only this were their house, they could hop into bed and take a nap?(hcbookpics.com/455)

- ☐ Remove extraneous furniture, leaving the bed, dresser, and night stands. You can even remove the dresser if you have space in your closet for items that it contains. Additional chairs are acceptable if there's a designated sitting area.
- ☐ Paint master bedroom a calm, neutral color/colors.
- ☐ Replace old sheets and bedding with white sheets and a white bedspread or comforter.
- ☐ Accent the white bedding with a aqua-blue or yellow throw.
- ☐ Remove all items from under the bed.
- ☐ Remove all medicines and other personal items from night stands.
- ☐ Place neutral-topic books on the night stands.
- ☐ Make sure that lights on the night stands are working properly.
- ☐ Place about seven colorful pillows of different sizes (with the largest in the back) on your bed to add visual interest. There should be more than your standard or king-sized pillows. They are primarily ornamental.
- ☐ Remove dog beds.
- ☐ Remove dog steps up to the bed.
- ☐ Make sure the drapes are clean.

☐ Use Rick's Rule 3: half and half again to reduce the number of items in the master closet.

☐ Confirm that all window blinds are functioning properly.

☐ Hang generic art pieces, such as photos of area scenery or abstract artwork.

☐ Add a live plant or flowers to the room.

☐ Make sure that window coverings match the bedding.

☐ Clean light switches.

☐ Make sure all light bulbs match and are working.

Secondary Bedrooms

Secondary bedrooms are traditionally children's or guest bedrooms. They need to look as large as possible. This is done by removing toys, extraneous furniture, and other items. Have children choose up to five of their favorite toys to play with, and put the remaining toys in easily accessible storage. If children want different toys, they need to trade them out. (hc-bookpics.com/460)

☐ Paint rooms a neutral color/colors.

☐ Remove extraneous furniture, leaving the bed, dresser, and night stands.

☐ Replace old sheets and bedding with new bedding that is light in color.

☐ Remove all items from under the bed(s).

☐ Use Rick's Rule 3 (half and half again) to reduce the number of items in the closets.

☐ Confirm that all window blinds are functioning properly.

☐ Hang generic art pieces, such as photos of area scenery or

abstract art.
- ☐ Make sure that window coverings match the bedding.
- ☐ Change room back to a bedroom setup from another use.
- ☐ Remove medicines from night stands.
- ☐ Add a small green plant to the night stand.
- ☐ Replace worn/dirty lamp shades.
- ☐ Confirm that lights/lamps/ceiling fan work.
- ☐ Clean light switches.
- ☐ Make sure all light bulbs match and are working.
- ☐ Vacuum the floor.

Bathrooms

You may have heard that kitchens and bathrooms sell houses. While I believe that may be an overstatement, these two room types are very important. The bathroom is often the first room that people go into in the morning, and the last room they are in at the end of the day. (hcbookpics.com/465)

You don't have to be a germaphobe to be grossed out by someone else's dirty bathroom. Remember Rick's Rule 2: Nobody wants to buy a used house? This rule applies to all rooms, but especially to bathrooms.

Alternatively, a bathroom can be a place where young children and parents have time to bond. When it is properly staged, it can be a place to relax and rejuvenate. Many high-end houses emphasize the spa-like master bathroom. This is because people want to relax in a jetted or even standard bathtub or stand under a "rain" shower head.

General

☐ Add new white or tan bath towels.

☐ Remove bath mats or rugs.

☐ Empty trash cans.

☐ Clean light switches.

☐ Make sure all light bulbs match and are working.

Vanity

☐ Remove all toiletries.

☐ Replace worn counter tops.

☐ Change outdated/worn faucets and drain cap.

☐ Make sure faucets are free of mineral deposits.

☐ Add a basket with rolled-up white or tan hand towels or washcloths.

☐ Add two lightly scented unlit candles.

Toilet

☐ If toilet is old or stained, replace with a higher-end toilet.

☐ Replace toilet seat with new one from hardware store.

☐ Remove hard-water stains.

☐ Clean toilet.

☐ Remove objects from tank.

☐ Keep lid and seat down.

Shower/Tub

☐ Clean thoroughly.

☐ Clean shower doors and/or curtain.

☐ Replace curtain if too dirty.

☐ Remove shampoo bottles and other shower items.

☐ Remove hard-water stains.

Rick Machle

☐ Replace soap with new bar.

Floors
☐ Wash floor.
☐ Vacuum the floor.
☐ Wash throw rugs, or replace if worn.
☐ Remove toilet plunger and scrub brush.
☐ Clean grout.

Stand-Alone Tub
☐ Clean thoroughly.
☐ Remove toiletries.
☐ Remove hard-water stains.
☐ Add basket of bath salts and scents
☐ Add new bar of soap.
☐ Add new scented unlit candles.
☐ Drape white or tan bath towels over the edge of the tub.

Mudroom

Mudrooms are a great space that parents love to store coats, boots, leashes and other items. This space should be presented as a great place to hang up items and sit to remove shoes. It needs to be neat and clean, so that a buyer can image the space keeping all of those items out the rest of the house - including the mud, dirt or sand that people track in. (hcbookpics.com/470)

☐ Remove all but a couple of coats.

☐ Remove shoes.

☐ Remove leashes.

☐ If your space does not have a space to sit, add one.

☐ Add Pillows to sitting area(s)

☐ Clean windows.

☐ Clean door.

☐ Clean rugs.

☐ Vacuum the floor.

☐ Wash floor.

Backyard

Your current back yard should be seen as an oasis from the outside world. Even if your back space is a small deck, balcony or patio, it should be as private and with as much greenery as possible. Even with small spaces there should be an area for relaxing and another for outdoor dining. If you have enough room, add a space for grilling. It's important for this area to be fresh and clean without tools, toys, pet waste or garden hoses lying around. (hcbookpics.com/475)

☐ Pick up pet waste.

☐ Pressure wash deck.

☐ Pressure wash patio.

☐ Re-stain or paint deck.

☐ Mow the lawn.

☐ Edge the lawn.

☐ Weed the garden(s).

☐ Rake leaves.

Holy *CRAP!* I'm Selling My Home. NOW WHAT?

- ☐ Pressure wash the fence.
- ☐ Wash glass door.
- ☐ Shovel snow from decks and patios.
- ☐ Make sure umbrellas are functioning.
- ☐ Put up umbrellas for showings unless it's too windy.
- ☐ Clean exterior (at least) of grill (remove cover for showings and photos).
- ☐ Clean seat cushions.
- ☐ Place outdoor pillows on seat cushions.
- ☐ Confirm that gas fireplace/fire pit are functioning.
- ☐ Clean outdoor fireplace, and replace with fresh wood.
- ☐ Stack wood next to fireplace.

Office/Study

A home office needs to be staged to convey that this is a space where you can get work accomplished, free from distractions. The layout can help this, as can removing unnecessary items. Often studies or offices can become multipurpose rooms. I have seen exercise equipment, cribs, sewing machines, and even huge TV's. While all of these could have been things that made the homeowners work more productively, it can be confusing to the buyer as to what this room is. Is it a study, exercise room, nursery, sewing room, or home theater? They need to know immediately that it's a study. (hcbookpics.com/480)

☐ Clean computer monitors.

☐ Remove papers.

☐ Dust the desk.

☐ Dust bookshelves.

☐ Dust other tables

- ☐ If you have a chair mat, make sure it's in good condition, or remove it if it is cracked or dented.
- ☐ Turn off computer.
- ☐ Set desk in the middle of the room with chair facing door.
- ☐ Clean light switches.
- ☐ Make sure all light bulbs match and are working.
- ☐ Vacuum the floor.

Rec Room

A rec room is an space for relaxing. This could be a room that's only large enough for a card table and small bar and place to watch TV. It could also be as large as many people's main floor with an area for a pool table, full bar, place to watch the 70" TV and even an indoor driving range. Whatever the size your space is (provided you have one), it should be staged similar to a sports bar. (hcbookpics.com/485)

☐ Remove extraneous items from bar.

☐ Clean the bar.

☐ Dust/clean pool tables.

☐ Rack up the pool table.

☐ Dust lights.

☐ Remove/organize toys.

☐ Clean light switches.

☐ Make sure all light bulbs match and are working.

☐ Vacuum the floor.

Wine Room/Cellar

There are homes with wine cellars, tasting rooms or space under the stairway that's cool for wine storage. These rooms need to be clean and organized. It's best to have all bottles in their storage compartments as opposed to having in boxes on the floor. (hcbookpics.com/488)

☐ Make sure all wine bottles are in the racks and not in boxes on the floor.

☐ Dust wine rack(s).

☐ Confirm that any refrigeration equipment is functioning properly.

☐ If there is a tasting area, set out a couple of wine glasses and ice bucket.

☐ Clean light switches.

☐ Make sure all light bulbs match and are working.

☐ Vacuum the floor.

Home Theater

When it's time for movie night or that big game, your buyer will want to see your home theater as a great place to watch TV or enjoy a good movie. It's also a great space to entertain in. Add movie posters and clean this space. To set the scene, consider a popcorn machine in one corner. (hcbookpics.com/490)

- ☐ Hang movie posters.
- ☐ Straighten up space.
- ☐ Confirm that any A/V equipment is functioning properly.
- ☐ Clean light switches.
- ☐ Make sure all light bulbs match and are working.
- ☐ Clean bar.
- ☐ Dust the sconce lights.
- ☐ Clean screen.
- ☐ Vacuum the floor.

Hot Tubs and Pools

Having a pool or hot tub can be an enticing addition to your property. This is only true if it is clean and in working condition. If it is not, it will be seen as a drawback to your home. It'll be something that the new buyer will have to deal with and not enjoy. If your hot tub is non-functional, have it removed before going on the market. A deck or pad with wiring ready for a hot tub is better than a broken hot tub in that space. (hcbookpics.com/495)

☐ Make sure all equipment is properly functioning.
☐ Clean hot tub and/or pool.
☐ Replace worn covers.
☐ Power wash decks.
☐ Clean and repair grout.
☐ Set out new or clean towels on chairs.
☐ Replace burned out lights.
☐ Wash the Deck

Workout/Exercise Room

Some people love to work out. Others of us do it because it is good for us. For those people, you want your exercise room or space to be trouble free. When your space is clean, picked up and gives the feeling that this is a place that is fun to workout in, potential buyers will see this space as an asset and could save them money because they won't have to join a gym. (hcbookpics.com/498)

☐ Organize equipment.

☐ Clean mirrors.

☐ Clean TV.

☐ Vacuum the floors.

☐ Clean floors.

☐ Make sure all light bulbs match and are working.

Look Good: Smell Good

Now that you have your house looking good, you need to remember that it needs to smell good too. The day before your showings, avoid cooking items that smell; meals like fish or heavy garlic dishes. Also, clean the cat box and pick up dog waste in the yard prior to showings to remove those odors. Empty the diaper pale as well. The hamster may need to go to grandma's home until your house is under contract. Refrain from smoking indoors for weeks before you sell. In Colorado and many other states, marijuana is legal, so many of the homes we photograph reek of pot. This isn't good if your potential buyer has a newborn baby. Professionally steam clean the carpets and floors to remove odors.

Now that you've removed items that can create odors, add back in some pleasant smells. These should be subtle. For safety DO NOT leave lighted candles throughout your house. There are safer alternatives. One option is to use plug-in air fresheners. Another is to use scent pods. Gold Canyon is a company that has a sugar cookie scent and oatmeal cookie. (hcbookpics.com/499). The pods require a warmer to activate the scents. Pod warmers come in many different styles to blend into your decor. The warmers come with an automatic shut off. You will have that just baked smell with no effort.

CHAPTER FIVE

Marketing to Set Your House Apart

In a seller's market, you and/or your agent need to market your house, to get the maximum price and multiple buyers. In a buyer's market, you need to market your house to get one buyer. When it comes to marketing and advertising your house, think of it as a product. It is a product in a very competitive environment. Buyers will have different criteria, such as location, square footage, style, features, and price. Regarding online searches, your house will need to fit into each of these to be found by specific buyers. Depending on the number of criteria the buyer types in, and the size of your community, there could be dozens—even hundreds of other properties directly competing with your house. You need to maximize the quality and exposure your house has in the marketplace. You want to make your house stand apart from the others through better marketing.

Media to Market Your Home

Photography

Great marketing begins with superior photography. Whether you are showing your house online, in print brochures or ads, or on social media, the photos will tell the story. Real estate photography is different from other types of photography. Even if your best friend is an awesome wedding and portrait photographer, that doesn't mean he or she should photograph your house. The way real estate photographers compose the photos, takes the photos, and processes them is completely different from most other types of photography. One quick way to determine if the photographer is a real estate photographer is if the walls are square to the sides of the photograph. There are two types of real estate photography: single exposure and High Dynamic Range (HDR) photos. (hcbookpics.com/500)

Single-Exposure Photography

Single-exposure photos are what most people traditionally take. You can typically tell if they are single exposure if the photographer is using a flash for indoor photos. This is the least expensive type because it is a way to photograph that is both quick to shoot and to process. The image quality is often good and has high contrast. Some sellers prefer this look to HDR photos, mainly because it's the way they have seen houses in photographs that they themselves have taken. (hcbookpics.com/505)

Here's the downside to single-exposure photography: to see the views out of the windows, you need to add bright strobe lights to equalize the light inside with the brighter light outside. Using a flash will create shadows that are not there the in the real world. For instance, if you have a chandelier above the dining room table, you'll now have a shadow on the ceiling. The lights will also show up in reflections in the windows, mirrors, or appliances.

One way to work around these issues is to shoot your photographs just before or after sunset. This way, the lighting between the inside and the outside is more equalized. Your house may have a warm glow, but most people prefer to have their houses look very bright when displayed online, which is difficult to achieve with twilight lighting.

HDR Photography

The solution to the limitations of single-exposure photography is the second type of photography, called HDR photography. HDR stands for "High Dynamic Range." Think of your eye as an HDR camera. Look at the corner of a window. You can see both what's outside of the window and the detail of the window frame and furniture on the inside. As previously described, a camera without a flash can expose the outside correctly, and the inside would be dark, or it can expose correctly for the inside, and the outside would be very bright, if not completely washed out. (hcbookpics.com/510)

With HDR photos, the photographer will take 3, 5, 7 or many more different images at various exposures from dark to light. Then those images are electronically superimposed over each other to build a composite image taking the best of each exposure. Most of the work in

HDR photography is done after the photographer leaves your house.

The term "HDR" only refers to the process just described. The final HDR photos can look anywhere from realistic to surrealistic. Some HDR images even look cartoonish. It all depends on how they are processed. When interviewing an agent, ask to see some of his or her photos from other houses the agent has listed. See if you like the way they look. Then look at those images online next to other photographs.

Here's what can be confusing. There are lots of companies who say, "Of course we do HD photos." Some are counting on you not knowing the difference between HD (high definition) and HDR (high dynamic range." HD usually denotes single exposures that measure at least 1920 X 1080 pixels. The superior photographs are HDR and not HD.

If your agent says he or she is using the HDR setting on a smartphone, be wary. While this is a similar process, the camera phone sensors are smaller, and images are grainier, which will make them inferior to those taken with professional equipment. The lenses that are used by professional photographers cost about as much as the entire smartphone, if not more. When these lenses are paired with a full-frame sensor, the photo shows more of the room without the distortion of a super wide-angle lens.

Some companies also use a computer program to

process your photos, and others use a professional photographer. If it's a computer, it will assume certain things like colors in that room. On the other hand, if a photographer is processing the photos, he or she is more likely to give an accurate representation of your house—especially if it's the photographer who took the photos. Once again, rely on your opinion of the photos you are seeing from your agent's other listings.

Don't let your photographer get too creative with the shots. A buyer has very little time to look at your house. You want buyers to be able to scroll though the rooms as quickly as possible. Go online and browse through various properties as if you were a buyer. Then, after this, think about how much time you spent on each house.

Many sellers will go online, look at their houses, and believe that prospects will simply hang out on your listing and look at every photograph. They won't. A prospect is someone who's looking at all the houses, and a buyer is specifically interested in your house. Once prospects have determined that your house might be what they are looking for, they will come back and take a more extensive look at your photos and other media. But you must get them hooked at first click. Up-close photos of the wrought-iron staircase or a creative shot of your rose bushes may just cause people to move onto the next house.

Every MLS has a limit to the number of photos allowed. Every shot needs to count. If you really need to have creative shots, put them at the end of all the photos that the MLS will allow you to add.

Aerial Photography

The word "drone" has become ubiquitous today. Packages might be delivered by drone; there are drones for the military, civilian law-enforcement uses, and wildfire evaluation, which are all great purposes. But for the right property, there's nothing better to show off its features than using aerial photography. (hcbookpics.com/515)

The use of drones, often called quadcopters, is a great way to show your house from a different vantage point.

Perhaps you live on a golf course or have open space in the back. By flying even thirty or forty feet above the ground, you can show off that space with your house in the foreground. You might live on a hillside with one level on the front and three on the back. A typical photograph of the back from the ground below the house would only show the underside of your decks. With the drone, you can fly up so that you can look straight on at the back of your house.

Of course, if you live on a large property of more than an acre or two, drones will be able to show the entire property. Buyers can even see that ocean beyond your house, or that great mountain view—that is, if you have one. Perhaps your house sits up from the street and has a wide or long driveway. From the ground, this shot becomes all about the driveway, and just going up ten or fifteen feet can minimize it and emphasize the house instead.

What if you live in an urban or suburban area? There are times when aerial photos simply are not appropriate. When houses are fifteen feet apart, aerial photos will just simply show how close they are to each other.

Aerial photos may also not make sense for a house with a great deal of foliage. Remember, if you have lots of trees, the higher you up you go, the less you will see of the house itself. The branches will obscure it. Look to see if there are any clearings in the trees where a drone can see your house clearly. Remember, if your house is in a northern climate and your trees are deciduous where the leaves fall off in the autumn, you may have better aerial shots during the fall and winter than during the summer. Of course, you may have to consider seeing brown grass and/or snow.

Most drones today have wide-angle lenses with minimal zoom capability. The wide angle will make objects like mountains or city scapes look farther away than they are in real life.

Simply because a person can fly a drone doesn't necessarily make him or her a good aerial photographer. It's more difficult than photography from the ground. On the ground it is important to think about where you put the camera and whether you should pan or move left or right. With aerial photography, you add the third up/down axis. The best photo may be just to the left of the house, but should it be at twenty-one feet or twenty-four feet? Those three feet can make the difference between a great aerial shot and an OK one.

Twilight Photographs

An exterior twilight photo is a great way to make your house stand out on the web. It brings the inside out by illuminating the windows and accenting the landscape. Of course, this assumes that you have a lot of windows on one side of your house. The best twilight photo could be from the front, the back, or the side. Perhaps you have a swimming pool or a hot tub that will show up really well at night. Of course, the best way to show off a fire pit is with a twilight photo. (hcbookpics.com/520)

Perhaps the photographer that you or the real estate agent is using doesn't know how to shoot HDR photography. As described earlier, shooting a house at dusk can work to equalize the lighting between the indoors and the outdoors. Some people like the look of the inside at dusk, but in my opinion, it's better to have your house look bright. This can only be accomplished by photographing the house during daytime.

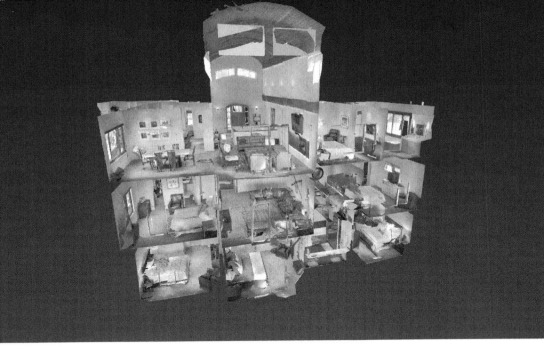

Virtual Tours

Ten to fifteen years ago, virtual tours were not only popular, but essential. That's because the photos that were on the MLS were quite small. The way to get around this was to create a virtual tour. Within the virtual tour, you could have photographs, links to other websites, all the details about the property (like bedrooms, bathrooms, and square footage). It was like having a listing within the listing.

Today, the world has changed. The MLS and other websites now have larger images. Now photos within the virtual tour are often smaller than what is in the MLS. What you'll find is that virtual tours are called "virtual" today because they are virtually not watched. There is one exception that we have found, and that is a special type of virtual tour called a Matterport®. (hcbookpics.com/535)

A Matterport® tour includes 360-degree images that are linked together so that you can virtually walk throughout your house. The most valuable aspect of Matterport® tours is that the buyer can see your entire house in three dimensions, like you would a doll house. There's also a floor-plan view with all the furniture that was in the house when it was photographed. There is an option to view the tour in VR mode using your smartphone and special visor. In this view, buyers can "stand" in your house, look around, and then move from room to room as if they were actually standing there in your property. If you haven't sold your house in the last few years, you probably don't even know this technology exists.

The advantage of a Matterport® tour is that it's giving your buyer the ability to walk throughout your house and take an open house tour twenty-four hours a day and from anywhere in the world. The images are extremely accurate, and the doll house and floor-plan views give your buyer the ability to view your house and see its layout. There are many other similar types of virtual-tour programs that allow you to walk throughout the house in 360-degree images, but the doll house and floor-plan views are unique to Matterport®.

Many of the online real estate websites like realtor.com prominently feature Matterport® tours on the main photographs for a house. We have found that each tour averages about one hundred unique visitors—or as we call them, "showings"—with 150 total visitors. Imagine having to get your house ready for one hundred showings. With Matterport®, you can get it ready once, and then only get it ready again for more serious buyers.

Video

When YouTube® started back in 2007, this began a great platform for real estate videos. There is not a cost for hosting the videos, but more importantly, it gives your house higher visibility within the Google® search engine. This is because Google® owns YouTube®. Videos can also be embedded as links in the MLS so that people can view them there as well. (hcbookpics.com/540)

When you go online, you will see two different types of real estate videos. One is essentially a slideshow of your photographs that were turned into a video. Perhaps there are additional graphics added to highlight special features, but the video is essentially your photos put to music. Because many of these videos are uploaded to YouTube at 720-pixel resolution, you end up with the same issue as virtual tours: the quality of the images is lower than that of the photos on the MLS. Why would people want to look through your house with a predetermined time line for each image when they can simply walk through the photos at their own pace? They wouldn't.

The second type of video is full-motion video. This can include video with music, where your home is highlighted using panning tilting and zooming shots. They can also include aerial video or more sophisticated smooth dolly shots through your house. This is a guided walk-through of your house. Put the most important features at the beginning of your video because most viewers will stop watching after the first two minutes.

The most enhanced videos include voice-over narration along with the full-motion video. The difference between a video and a Matterport® is the video is like you walking someone through your house, while the Matterport® is like you leaving and letting the buyers walk around your home at their leisure. Both have their purposes when selling real estate. Another great use for videos is to post them on social media like Twitter®, Facebook® and Instagram®.

Online Marketing

MLS

The most important marketing tool available to market your house is the Multiple Listing Service, or MLS. The information contained here will be spread throughout the internet. It is also where other agents turn to find out about your house and whether it is what their buyers are looking for.

The information described in the public remarks will tell the buyer what makes your house special. It also contains other detailed specifications about your house, as well as the price. In the non-public data, agents will also be able to see the price history. If you have had four price drops in the past eight weeks, the other agents will be able to see it. Therefore, pricing your home correctly is very important. Whether you are selling your home yourself or with an agent, be sure to proof the details like number of bedrooms and bathrooms and square footage. These are also common search criteria.

Once the data and photos are put into the MLS, it will then be syndicated to other real estate websites throughout the internet.

Internet

It's all about the internet. You want your house to be on as many websites as possible. You never know which website a buyer will be browsing on. If all the other houses that are for sale in your community are on a website and yours is not, it's as if your house isn't even for sale. Even if you're selling your house as a "for sale by owner," you'll want to have your house in the MLS as well as on all the websites. There are companies that will do this for a minimal fee. However, don't expect other services alongside this.

You want these websites to have enough information to give the buyer a good idea of what your house is like. Having excellent photos and a quality virtual tour will give you a leg up on other properties that don't.

Social Media

I'm not sure that you've heard, but there are companies named Facebook®, Instagram® and Twitter® that are dominating the media today. Many people are use these social media platforms to share with friends and family, everything that's going on in their lives. If your house isn't being talked about either from you to your friends or from your agent to his or her sphere, or both, then you're potentially missing a huge number of people, one of whom could be the buyer of your house.

A social media post is different from a virtual tour or video where you can tell every detail about your house. On those you only have one shot to tell your story. With social media, you want to have several postings about your house. Perhaps the agent will talk about your kitchen on one post. Another post could be about your wonderful back deck, patio or yard. A third one could be about that spa-like master bathroom. Not every Facebook post is seen by every person who is his or her "friend." In fact, most are not. Therefore, you need multiple posts. Be sure that the agent shares these posts with you, so that you can share them on your time line or feed as well. Short videos on Instagram are great way to tease your property. Make sure they are Tweeted as well.

Print

Were this book written twenty years ago, print would be the first part of this chapter. Back then, website photos were low-quality, and the photos were very small. Pages took forever to load because of slower internet connection speeds. Today more than 90 percent of all buyers start their searches on the web. This means that they're not usually going to find your house in a newspaper or magazine ad. Unless you're very lucky, they're not going to buy your house from the brochure box out front either.

While print is typically not the primary source for attracting your buyer, it shouldn't be ignored either. You want high-quality brochures out front and in the house on the kitchen counter, so buyers can make notes and take them with them.

Likewise, print advertising falls under the "leave no stone unturned" category. The issue with most print advertising is that there's a delay from the time your information is submitted and when it goes to press. If you're in a sellers' market, even waiting until this weekend for it to be seen can be too late for that potential buyer. Magazine ads can take even longer to go to press; you never know what the market will do. Therefore, you probably want to have print advertising as well just in case that is where your potential buyer is looking.

In-Person Marketing

Open Houses

You may be asking why an open house is the last entry on the list of marketing tools. The best was not saved for last. While this is something that nearly everyone believes is a good way to market your house, it is not. A recent small survey of agents found that over half of the agents that hold open houses do it for two reasons: to get more clients or to show you that they are working to sell your house. One definition of a successful open house is that a lot of people come to see your house. How many are neighbors? How many are real buyers? How many are there to steal from you? If you have a lot of people walking through your house, how many can one agent watch at a time? This is a good opportunity to remind you to lock up or remove all valuables and prescription medicines. If you value it, then it should be removed from your house. Do this whether it is an open house or a showing.

There is also another type of open house called a broker open. This is a good open house where your agent will invite other agents to your house. You will find that a broker open is a good way for other buyers through their agents to see your house. Instead of the general public going through your house, you will have agents going through. Because they are now familiar with your house, these agents can point potential buyers your direction. It is difficult for a seller who is not working with an agent to hold a broker open. This is also when it is good to have an agent who is part of a larger company or office. Often the agents will be in and out in a couple of minutes, but that is enough for them to get a feel for your house.

CHAPTER 6

Pricing It Right

While the marketing programs described in the previous chapter are important, having your house priced correctly is critical. There are three parts to getting a successful offer. You need to market your home which is worth 25 percent. You market your home to attract the maximum number of potential buyers. Marketing programs with attract the right person at the right time. This is worth 24 percent. The third part is the price. It equals 51 percent. Notice that this is worth more than the other two combined.

You can do all the marketing perfectly, and the right person can find your house because of that marketing, but if the price is too high, your house will not go under contract. In other words, this book Is being written to assist you in attracting the right buyer by marketing it correctly, but the most important aspect of marketing is having your house priced correctly.

Price is so important that if you decide to price your house below market, you will probably not have to do much marketing, including staging, because word will get out, and the right person will find your house just because it's priced way below market. However, you'll be leaving money on the table. There may be circumstances that require you to do this. An effective marketing strategy to sell your house quickly is to have a price that looks like a deal, but not so low that buyers will wonder whether there is something wrong with the property.

Set the price too high, and your house could sit on the market too long. Set it too low, and you're leaving money behind.

One pricing strategy is to price your house slightly below market. This should attract multiple buyers. With multiple buyers, and the right market conditions, you could have a bidding war.

Another strategy is to price your house slightly higher than market. You may elect to do this because your house has many more upgrades compared to the surrounding houses. Just remember Rick's Rule 5: it doesn't matter what you paid. This strategy requires that you be ready to lower your price quickly if you don't find that you're having showings or you're not getting offers. You don't want to creep down, but make a significant price reduction. If you move down slowly, it could take a long time to get to the market price. That could give people the impression that your property has issues other than it as not priced correctly. Market conditions could also change, and you are now chasing the market down. If you start out high and then quickly move to the market price that your agent probably indicated should be the initial price, then the market will realize that it was an incorrect initial price.

Pricing your house even a few hundred or thousand dollars too high can result in some online buyers never seeing it. For instance, you decide that your house should be $304,900. If someone is looking for a property up to $300,000, that person would never pull up your house. Think of putting your house at $300,000. Perhaps a buyer is looking for a house from $200,000 to $300,000. Your house would then meet their search criteria. Likewise, a different buyer could find your house if he or she is looking in the $300,000 to $400,000 price range.

Don't be insulted by low offers. Some buyers who present low offers are known as "bottom-feeders." These are buyers or investors looking for distressed sellers wanting to sell at low prices. Other buyers are testing whether you'd be willing to sell for much less than the market. With either of these buyers, you should counter their offers—perhaps slightly lower than your current price. This counter will indicate that you're willing to negotiate but that you aren't desperate. The bottom-feeder will probably start searching elsewhere. The serious buyer may make a counter to your counter. Either you'll come to an agreement on price and terms or you won't. Even so, you'll have more information about whether your price is correct.

How long your house is on the market can affect its price. The measurement is called "days on market." The longer your property is on the market, the more it can cost you. The number of days on market can be impacted by time of year, overall market conditions, the property's condition, and the price. A house priced well above the average sales price for your area will probably take longer to sell. This is because the buyer pool is smaller. It is not uncommon for some properties to have seven hundred days on market.

There are some real estate websites that will give you an estimate as to the value of your house. An estimate from these sites should be considered that - an estimate. Often these sites use public data to estimate the value of your house based on size, bedrooms, bathrooms, etc. It is also based on similar homes. What is less precise are the condition of your house, upgrades that you or other sellers made, and the time of year you are trying to sell. Use these estimates as a data point, but your value may or may not be significantly different based on your particular circumstances.

Timing Is Everything

During a normal real estate market in the United States, there are many more buyers in spring and early summer. Of course, you'll probably have more competition as there are more houses for sale as well. In the winter you'll have less competition for your property, but fewer buyers.

The market is not always normal. Market conditions can affect your price as well. Suppose you decided to sell in the early spring of 2008. You priced your house higher than others in your neighborhood throughout the spring and summer. Now it is October of 2008, at the start of the Great Recession. You're going to be selling for significantly less than what you would have in the spring if it were priced correctly. During 2008 and 2009, the market value in many states dropped by 50 percent. While this is an extreme example of what can happen, it does exemplify how the market can change. You don't want to be "smarter" than you really are. Remember, market conditions are only clear in the rearview mirror. Some sellers try to be eager in the spring to push the price, but don't adjust the price quickly enough, so by the time that they do in mid- to late summer, they have missed the peak.

Not only can the time of year affect the price, but the day of the week is important too. You'll probably want to put your house on the market on Thursday or Friday. You want your property to be "hot" for the weekend.

Don't forget about holidays. Unless your personal circumstances require it, you probably don't want to put your property on the market during low-traffic periods. These typically include long weekends that surround holidays. If you put your house on the market the Friday before Labor Day weekend, you might have just added seven days to your days on market. This is because buyers may not start looking at your house until the Friday or Saturday after the holiday. Putting your house on the market in early December could mean there will not be serious buyers until after the holidays in mid-January. Now you have added thirty to forty-five days to your days on market. You may want to get everything ready in December but wait to put it on the market until mid-January. Remember to take photos of your house before putting up holiday decorations so that your house does not look dated when it goes on the market.

Interest Rates and Price

Interest rates can also affect your price. Since the Great Recession, interest rates have either been flat or going down.

Rick Machle

This means that buying power has been positively impacted by interest rates. In recent years rates have begun to go back up. For every 1 percent rate increase, the buying power goes down about 10 percent. This factor can make it impossible for some buyers to qualify for your house. The buyer will need to come up with cash to cover the difference. If the buyer doesn't have the cash, he or she will now have to look for a house that is priced lower than yours. You may also now need to lower the price of your house to attract the same buyer pool that was available when rates were lower.

Here's an example. A buyer qualifies for a thirty-year mortgage for a $300,000 house at 4.5 percent interest rate. The monthly payments would be $1,520. This is the maximum amount this buyer can qualify for. Now, interest rates rise to 5.5 percent; the most this buyer can now afford is $268,250. Unless you're willing to drop your price by over $30,000, this is no longer a potential buyer. The only other option is for you or the buyer to buy down that interest rate by buying down points. How much this will cost depends on the value of the house. Speak to a qualified mortgage lender to find out more about buying down points.

Whatever price you choose, you need to be ready to move quickly to react to the market.

CHAPTER 7

Relax.
Be Patient.
Be Flexible.

Having made it through this book, you deserve a bonus Rick's Rule.

Rick's Rule 6: One word makes all the difference.

Changing a single word from "have" to "get," as in "have to" to "get to," can make this process go so much smoother. This rule works not only when selling your house but also for anything else in your life that you don't want to do. For instance, what if you told yourself that you "get" to exercise instead of "have" to exercise. No longer is this task considered a chore, but rather a choice that you are making to reach the ultimate goal. Instead of "I have to clean out my closets," tell yourself "I get to clean out my closets." Make it an opportunity to declutter your house and life. Tell yourself "I get to paint the house" instead of "I have to paint the house." Change "I have to clean out the garage." to "I get to clean out the garage." Lucky for you now you "get" to relax, be patient and flexible.

Now that you have come to the end of this book, you are ready to get started. Once you have decided whether you want someone to assist you in selling your house (and if so, who that is), determined a beginning list price, prepared your home for sale, and set up the marketing tools that you are going to use, you can now simply wait for the right buyer to come forward and buy your house. It's time for you to sit back and trust the process, trust the market and trust the person that you may have hired to represent you as well.

You also need to be prepared to make changes. As soon as you go on the market and have a few showings, you should start getting feedback about your property. Ideally, the feedback is "I want to buy your house." Short of that, you need to listen to the input and, when possible, make changes based on those suggestions. Sometimes the suggestions can't be made. For instance, you may live on a busy road. Obviously, there is nothing you can do about that. But if it is something like "Wow, that's wild paint in the living room," you can respond by painting the living room with a neutral color.

It is possible that you are not able or willing or financially able to make some changes. You may instead decide to lower the price to encourage your buyer to overlook them. For $10,000, a buyer might be willing to purchase your house even if it has 1980's brass faucets throughout. However, you may find that it's less expensive to change out the faucets and modernize the house. This change could also result in a higher offer price by attracting a different buyer or buyers.

Over the years, there's one piece of advice that agents consistently share. Sellers who are flexible and willing to react quickly to what the market is telling them about their prices are more likely to sell their houses and therefore be much less stressed. When your agent tells you to lower your price, you need to ask why and then be willing to listen to the suggestion. Instead of lowering it all the way to where the agent wants, you may come to an agreement that it should be lowered a smaller amount for now. If you don't see sufficient action or receive an offer you then must agree to lower the price the rest of the way after a predetermined period. Be ready to act even faster if you see market conditions moving quicker.

You started out this book thinking, "Holy crap! I'm selling my home. Now what?" And as we've walked through the process, you are probably now saying, "What's the big deal? I've got this."

Good luck with the sale of your house! At times you may find it stressful. Just keep in mind that pot of gold at the end of the closing. Everything else will seem minor. Speaking of miners (pun intended), 150 years ago, many settlers in the United States traveled three thousand miles in covered wagons in hopes of finding a few flakes of gold. Relatively speaking, the work you need to do is easy. Time to polish up that pile of gold that you sleep in every night and wait for someone to buy it.

Made in the USA
Middletown, DE
27 January 2022